THE PRODIGAL
A Spiritual Retreat

The Prodigal: A Spiritual Retreat Copyright© 2023 Herbert F. Lamp, Jr. and Deborah J. Lamp.

ISBN 979-8-9882622-0-6

All Scripture quotations, unless otherwise indicated, are taken from the Holy Bible, New International Version®, NIV®. Copyright ©1973, 1978, 1984, 2011 by Biblica, Inc.™ Used by permission of Zondervan. All rights reserved worldwide. www.zondervan.com The "NIV" and "New International Version" are trademarks registered in the United States Patent and Trademark Office by Biblica, Inc.™

Scripture quotations taken from the (NASB®) New American Standard Bible®, Copyright © 2020 by The Lockman Foundation. Used by permission. All rights reserved. lockman.org

Cover and Inside Images: Rembrandt van Rijn's *The Return of the Prodigal Son*

Edited by Stacey Covell at One Word Editing, www.OneWordEditing.com

Cover and Interior Design by Sarah O'Neal at Eve Custom Artwork, www.evecustomartwork.com

The PRODIGAL
A Spritual Retreat

For Individual & Group Retreats

HERBERT F. LAMP, JR.
DEBORAH J. LAMP

The Digital Companion

The Prodigal: A Spiritual Retreat Digital Companion was created to allow the links to music, video and a full color graphics more readily accessible. Whether for group or individual participants, the Digital Companion makes participation easy. Throughout the retreat there are directives to look closely at certain areas of the painting or to "Play the Song" and with the Digital Companion, all you need is right at your fingertips.

Available Online

For use on iPad or Kindle

amazonkindle

The apostles gathered around Jesus and reported to him all they had done and taught. Then, because so many people were coming and going that they did not even have a chance to eat, he said to them, "Come with me by yourselves to a quiet place and get some rest."

Mark 6:30–31

The Guide

BEFORE WE BEGIN

Getting Away: Time & Length	x
Getting Away: Location	xi
Getting Away: Alone or in a Group Together	xii
Getting Away: Theme of the Retreat	xiii
Schedule	xiv
Getting Away: Material Needed	xv
Finally	xvi

THE RETREAT

Opening	3
Liturgy for Gathering	4
Vizio Divina	8
Introduction to Prodigal Retreat	12
Excerpt from The Cross & The Prodigal	13

THE YOUNGER SON

The Younger Son – Release	27
The Open/Closed Fist Exercise	30
Reflect & Ponder	32
Debrief	39

THE ELDER SON — 40

The Elder Son – Receive	41
Breath Prayer Exercise	44
Reflect & Ponder	45
Debrief	53

MEAL BREAK

THE FATHER

The Father — Rest	56
Resting in the Love of the Father Exercise	59
Reflect & Ponder	60
Closing	67
Reflect & Share	68
The Liturgy of Leave Taking	69

NOTES	71
BIBLIOGRAPHY	73
DISCOGRAPHY	73

Before We Begin

GETTING AWAY

[handwritten: doing is good - what we focus on is very important.]

When was the last time you gave intentional attention to your spiritual life and practices? Specifically, how recently have you really taken the time—a few hours, a day, weekend, or week—to pause your daily activities, temporarily set aside your obligations, concerns, and your frantic schedule to focus less on *doing* and more on *being*, especially being with God? *[handwritten: Human being]*
In our fast-paced lives full of responsibilities and distractions, the thought of putting everything on hold, even for a few hours, and spending time designed for spiritual renewal can feel out of the question. And even if we do, how exactly are we to spend listen. Without cultivating our interior lives, we lose touch with the one thing that should mean the most to us in this life: our relationship to God.

Ruth Haley Barton, in her book, *Invitation to Retreat*, discusses how we often use word retreat in the same way the military uses the term, which is used as a tactical withdrawal to recover in battle and then reengage the enemy. A military retreat can be a wise move. As Barton says, "there are times when we too need to pull back from the battle lines in our own lives rather than continuing to fight the same battles in the same ways. We need to pull back from our busyness, from life in our culture, from other people's expectations and our own compulsions, from whatever is not working in our lives."[1]

The great news is that the decision to retreat does not need to be just one more thing to add to our to-do list. We have created a simple one-day spiritual retreat guide to help you plan and implement your next time away with the Lord. We hope that by using this guide for a facilitated retreat, either with a group or on your own, you will find one less barrier toward making the time and hearing from God happen.

To have uninterrupted time and space to get away, we also need to deal with the organization of such a retreat. Four considerations need attention when planning this retreat.

Getting Away :: Time & Length

The first thing to consider in having a retreat is space and time. While we encourage people to give adequate time to a retreat, for many, taking more than one day is a genuine obstacle to getting away. Due to time and cost, you might not be able to do more than just a day with no overnight. Therefore, we have designed this retreat simply for this amount of time (one day). However, if you are fortunate enough to have more time, you can tailor the retreat by adding more time into the suggested schedule. As written, we are suggesting an hour for individual reflection time for each section of the retreat. However, if you want to extend the retreat into multiple days, you can easily add extra reflection time to each section based on your own preferences. Thus, you can make it a two-day retreat or even a week-long one.

For example, if you want to have a week-long retreat, we suggest you designate a single day to each section to encompass three out of the five days away. The other two days can be time alone with God, with no facilitated guidelines. You can spend that time taking a hike, journaling your thoughts, reading scripture or a delightful book, listening to and singing worship music, or simply napping. Whatever works for you—just be in it.

Getting Away :: Location

In addition to deciding on the amount of time you will spend on your retreat, the question of where you retreat is also important. If possible, take the opportunity to leave your home and venture out to a quiet and solitary space. For most people, that usually means a place where you will not be interrupted and somewhere close to nature. Since you will be doing some reading and writing, having good lighting and a table or a comfortable place to read and write will be helpful. Severe weather and other weather conditions can be a problem, so also take weather into account as you plan your retreat.

If you only have a day and cannot go anywhere else—a day at home is possible. We suggest removing as many distractions as possible. For example, turn off your phone and electronics, decide on a simple and already prepared meal, and try to be alone at home if possible. Hopefully, you will be able to adjust your day so you will have the space and change of pace to your daily rhythms during your time of retreat.

Finally, part of limiting distractions for your day away is honoring your commitments to other people. To make sure you can be fully present with the Lord, it would be good, as much as possible, to plan to have met your commitments to family and ministry while you are away. Of course, if you wait until all commitments are met, you will never retreat. So, we advise on planning ahead as best as you are able, but also encourage you not to let it become the reason you do not retreat. Blocking off the day on your calendar and making key people aware that you will not be available will be important. Some people find marking their email as "Out of Office" also helps to eliminate that distraction.

Getting Away :: *Alone or in a Group Together*

You can use this retreat guide in a group setting or in a personal setting with minor adjustments. The main difference being during the sharing time. Obviously, if you are alone, you cannot share what the Lord has been inviting you into with anyone else. So, we suggest you use the sharing time to journal or record your insights about what the Lord has been revealing during your reflective times. Then, when you return to your normal routine, we encourage you to share your insights with someone else at that time.

Whether sharing with someone during the retreat or later on, sharing with another person is a crucial factor in cementing what the Lord has been revealing to you. Make sure however, that whomever you share with is a safe and confidential person. If you are uncomfortable with sharing about your retreat experience with another person, then just talk to God and tell him what you are experiencing. Capturing your feelings and thoughts is helpful in remembering what God has shown you after you reengage with normal life again.

Getting Away :: Theme of the Retreat

We have formed our retreat around the three stages of Christian life that classic Christian spirituality has traditionally taught: ***purgation, illumination,*** and ***union.*** The first stage is called ***purgation,*** where the Christian disciple encounters God and renounces their past life of blatant sins, willful disobedience, and comes into a greater trust of God's goodness. Next is ***illumination,*** which is the active discipline of total consecration to God in love. A person experiences God through an integration of being, increased prayer life, and increased social awareness. The final stage is ***union,*** where the person experiences abiding in Christ by total abandonment to grace and resting in God's love.

While purgation, illumination, and union are traditional terms, they are also archaic and can be easily misunderstood today. Therefore, for the purposes of our retreat, we will instead use the terms ***release, receive,*** and ***rest. Release,*** as seen in the parable of the prodigal, represents the younger son's spiritual need (purgation). ***Receive*** represents the elder son's spiritual need (illumination). And finally, we experience the Father's love through ***rest*** (union).

We have designed this retreat and use this terminology based upon the parable of the prodigal son from Luke 15:11–32. We have found this parable to be a great illustration of the classic spiritual path. Following the framework of Henri Nouwen's spiritual classic, ***The Return of the Prodigal Son,*** the day is divided into three sections: the younger son (release); the elder son (receive); and the Father (rest). Below is the proposed schedule for a one-day retreat. Please feel free to adjust the schedule to fit your own needs. Overall, the retreat should take about seven hours from start to finish. But this may vary according to the size of the group. The more people attending, the more time will be needed for group sharing. In the pages that follow, we will explain each section and provide both the teaching notes and reflective questions.

9 a.m.	**Welcomes & Introductions** *especially for group retreats*
9:15 a.m.	**Gathering** | Liturgy for Gathering; Worship Song; Vizio Divina; Introduction to the Day
9:45 a.m.	**The Younger Son – Release** | *Luke 15:11–32* | Teaching on the Younger Son — Release; Open/Closed Fist Exercise
10:00 a.m.	**Time Alone with God** | Reflections on the Younger Son Releasing to the Father
11:00 a.m.	**Gathering to Share**
11:30 a.m.	**The Elder Son – Receive** | *Luke 15:11–32* | Teaching on The Elder Son — Receive; Breathe Prayer Exercise
11:45 a.m.	**Time Alone with God** | Reflections on the Elder Son Receiving from the Father
12:45 p.m.	**Gathering to Share**
1:15 p.m.	**Silent Meal Break & Rest**
2:00 p.m.	**The Father – Rest** | *Luke 15:11–32* | Teaching on the Father Rest; Drawing Exercise
2:15 p.m.	**Time Alone with God** | Reflections on the Father's Love — Rest
3:15 p.m.	**Gathering to Share** | Giving of Hearts
3:45 p.m.	**Liturgy of Leave Taking**

Schedule

Getting Away :: Material Needed

As we engage in the retreat material, we will use different methods of listening to and with God. If meeting as a group, we encourage you to have the following material on hand for all participants.

First, encourage those coming to bring their Bibles, something to write with, and journals. We feel unplugging is good for the soul, so we discourage attendees from using their phones and other electronics during the retreat.

MATERIALS

- *A large print of Rembrandt's painting The Return of the Prodigal Son*
- *A board or flip chart and means of attaching the print to it. An empty space on a nearby wall can work as well.*
- *A smaller, individual print of Rembrandt's painting for each participant*
- *Pens and sharpies*
- *A box of colored pencils for each participant*
- *Two name tags for each participant*
- *A small stone heart for each participant. (Available on Amazon.) Other materials can be used for the hearts as available and desired.*
- *A portable sound system*
- *This retreat guide for each participant*

Finally

As we contemplate the retreat experience, it is important to remember the desire is that we return to our lives and to others after the retreat with greater strength and joy. This is accomplished most significantly by just being in God's presence. If we get caught up in trying to stay too rigid with schedule or content, we might miss what God is inviting us into during our time with Him.

While we have provided a guided retreat, we encourage you to listen to the invitations God sends your way through the Holy Spirit during your time with Him, which may or may not be related to the material presented here. As Ruth Haley Barton so aptly puts it: "Nothing I could do for myself even approaches what God can do for me in the context of retreat."[2]

As we learn to release what controls our heart and keeps us distant from God, as we learn to receive all that God wants to give to us, and when we learn to simply rest in His love, we hope this retreat will be just what was needed. We pray this time away will allow you to return and fully engage in your active and present lives with fuller vigor and stronger love.

The RETREAT

The Retreat

GATHERING

Opening

After welcoming everybody and making the introductions and announcements for the day, let's start our time together and with the Lord by offering a prayer of gathering. The facilitator of the retreat will take the part of leader and everyone else will read the "All" lines.

Liturgy for Gathering

he was lost and is found.

Leader: We come as we are Loving God, to spend time in corporate solitude and to rest in you today.

All: *We bring with us all sorts of things that occupy our minds and take our energy, hopes, fears, tasks, and tears, the trivial and the overwhelming details of the day.*

Leader: Help us to approach this time with confidence, knowing that you desire our healing and our holiness.

All: *Help us to begin to look at what we hold tightly, at what we are afraid to relinquish into your love. Help us to look at what we need to receive from your good and generous hand and to realize that you have always been with us and everything you have is ours if we just ask. And help us to find complete rest in our Father's love, knowing that by completely abiding in you we are free from worry and fear.*

Leader: We thank you Father of all, that you are the giver of good gifts. May we recognize and name the things you want to birth in us, new possibilities, new hopes, and new life.

All: *Father God, sometimes we struggle with the changes that we must endure before you can bring this new life to us, before we can take new life out into our families and communities. Help us to name our doubts honestly before you in the prayerful expectation of receiving from your hand your gifts to us today.*

Leader: We thank you that you offer us a permanent home within your love, a home where we can feel safe, accepted, and free to grow into the people you created us to be and into the rest that resides in you.

All: *Homemaker God, help us to explore the rest you have prepared for us in Christ Jesus. As we step aside from the busyness which clouds our vision of your glory, may your Holy Spirit reveal to us the depth and breadth of your love for us. Amen.*3

He says, "Be still, and know that I am God;

I will be exalted among the nations,

I will be exalted in the earth."

Psalm 41:10

Worship

We will continue with our opening by singing or listening to a worship song to prepare our hearts to receive the Word.

PLAY THE SONG — *If you are alone, you may want to pick your own song(s) to worship along with. For groups, we have selected "Be Still and Know," by Steven Curtis Chapman.*

We will end our time of opening worship by having the leader slowly pray aloud Psalm 46:10, pausing at the end of each line for approximately five seconds.

PRAYER :: PSALM 41:10

Be still and know that I am God

Be still and know that I am

Be still and know

Be still

Be

Amen

Vizio Divina

Vizio Divina is Latin for "divine seeing." It is related to the prayer form of Lectio Divina (divine reading) but instead of Scripture, this form of prayer uses visual elements. We prayerfully invite God to speak to our hearts as we look at an image.

> **GROUP** | *Display the large poster of Rembrandt's The Return of the Prodigal Son.*
> **INDIVIDUAL** | *Please refer to the picture provided here, on the cover or in the Digital Companion.*

Before you begin, take a few moments to center upon the Lord, inviting the Holy Spirit to speak to your heart through what you see, with no agenda. This may occur through words, thoughts, or emotions.

Now, set your eyes on the painting, taking in the whole of it, its form, color, mood, patterns, light, shapes, lines, texture. Allow your vision to rest on the image and soak it in.

> **GROUP** | *People may want to gather around the painting to better view it.*

The Return of the Prodigal Son *is an oil painting by Rembrandt van Rijn, part of the collection of the Hermitage Museum in St. Petersburg. It is among the Dutch master's final works, likely completed within two years of his death in 1669. Art historian, Kenneth Clark claimed it is the greatest picture ever painted. See John I. Durham, The Biblical Rembrandt, 183.*

PONDER

What do you notice in the painting?

Where are your eyes drawn to? What might that mean?

What emotions does it evoke as you view it?

If you had to describe the painting in a sentence or two, what would you say?

Picture yourself walking around in the painting.
If you were in it, where would you be?

If you were one of the people in the painting, who might you be?

Take a few moments for quiet reflection. Record your observations.

GROUP | *Share your insights prompted by the questions asked above.*

Introduction to Prodigal Retreat

The parable of the prodigal son, also called *Evangelium in Evangelio*, or the gospel within the Gospel, is one of the most powerful stories Jesus ever told.[4] Kenneth E. Bailey has skillfully described the Gospel message in the parable by putting forth a cluster of theological themes which is held together by the story.[5] For added background we have included his description of these themes at the end of this section.

Jesus's parable tells the story of two sinners; the younger son who is a lawbreaker and the elder son who is a law-keeper. Each son represents a broken relationship with the father. The younger son breaks the relationship with his father by rejecting him and failing to meet the expectations of society and family. While the elder son meets those expectations, he yet breaks the relationship with family and father through his refusal to welcome back his brother.

The Return of the Prodigal Son, by Henri Nouwen, focuses on the three main characters in the story, the younger son, the elder son, and the Father, and how we might be like each of them. The following questions can help us to meditate on these characters and how we might relate to them. First, how do we resemble the younger son who initially rejected the Father only then to come back home? Second, how are we like the elder son in resenting his younger brother and his father's acceptance of his return? And finally, how are we challenged to love as the Father loves?

This three-fold study of younger son, elder son, and Father echoes the classic spiritual formation pattern of ***purgation, illumination,*** and ***union*** or as previously discussed release, receive, and rest to indicate the younger son's need to ***release*** (that of going his own way and prideful living), the elder son's need to ***receive*** (all the goodness the Father wants to give him), and our need to ***rest*** in our Father's love (to abide in Him).

Excerpt from The Cross & The Prodigal

> The Parable of the Two Lost Sons — the Theological Cluster

SIN | The parable exhibits two types of sin. One is the sin of the law-breaker and the other the sin of the law-keeper. Each centers on a broken relationship. One breaks the relationship while failing to fulfill expectations of the family and society. The second breaks the relationship while fulfilling those same expectations.

FREEDOM | God grants ultimate freedom to humankind, which is the freedom to reject his love. Humankind is free to choose its own way even if that causes infinite pain to the loving heart of God.

REPENTANCE | Two types of repentance are dramatically illustrated: (1) earn your acceptance as a servant/craftsman, (2) accept the costly gift of being found as a son/daughter.

GRACE | Grace is freely offered love that seeks and suffers in order to save.

JOY | For the father, joy is in finding. For the son, joy is in being found and restored to community.

FATHERHOOD | The image of God as a compassionate father is here given its finest definition in all of Scripture. That definition includes the offer of costly love to law-breakers and to law-keepers.

SONSHIP | Each son returns to the father either defining (the older son) or intending to define (the prodigal) his relationship to the father as that of a servant before a master. The father will not accept this definition. He offers costly love to each, out of his determination to have sons responding to love rather than merely servants obeying commands.

CHRISTOLOGY | Twice the father takes upon himself the form of a suffering servant who in each case offers a costly demonstration of unexpected love. ... There is a dramatic "self-emptying" in each case. The third parable embodies an implied one-to-one relationship between the actions of Jesus and the actions of the father in that each welcomes sinners into table fellowship. This unity of action affirms a unity of person.

FAMILY/COMMUNITY | The father offers costly love to his sons in order to restore them to fellowship in the context of a family or community. The family is Jesus' metaphor for the church.

INCARNATION & ATONEMENT | The father empties himself and goes down and out to meet the sons where they are (incarnation). In the process he demonstrates costly redeeming love (atonement). ...

EUCHARIST | As he partakes in the banquet the prodigal is sitting and eating with the father who through self-giving love won the prodigal into fellowship with himself. ... The mood of the banquet/Eucharist is that of a celebration. ...

ESCHATOLOGY | The messianic banquet has begun. All who accept the father's costly love are welcome as his guests. Table fellowship with Jesus is a proleptic celebration of the messianic banquet of the end times.[6]

The Story

The Parable of the Lost Son
Luke 15:11-32

11 Jesus continued: "There was a man who had two sons. 12 The younger one said to his father, 'Father, give me my share of the estate.' So he divided his property between them.

13 "Not long after that, the younger son got together all he had, set off for a distant country and there squandered his wealth in wild living. 14 After he had spent everything, there was a severe famine in that whole country, and he began to be in need. 15 So he went and hired himself out to a citizen of that country, who sent him to his fields to feed pigs. 16 He longed to fill his stomach with the pods that the pigs were eating, but no one gave him anything.

17 "When he came to his senses, he said, 'How many of my father's hired servants have food to spare, and here I am starving to death! 18 I will set out and go back to my father and say to him: Father, I have sinned against heaven and against you. 19 I am no longer worthy to be called your son; make me like one of your hired servants.' 20 So he got up and went to his father.

"But while he was still a long way off, his father saw him and was filled with compassion for him; he ran to his son, threw his arms around him and kissed him.

21 "The son said to him, 'Father, I have sinned against heaven and against you. I am no longer worthy to be called your son.'

22 "But the father said to his servants, 'Quick! Bring the best robe and put it on him. Put a ring on his finger and sandals on his feet. 23 Bring the fattened calf and kill it. Let's have a feast and celebrate. 24 For this son of mine was dead and is alive again; he was lost and is found.' So they began to celebrate.

25 "Meanwhile, the older son was in the field. When he came near the house, he heard music and dancing. 26 So he called one of the servants and asked him what was going on. 27 'Your brother has come,' he replied, 'and your father has killed the fattened calf because he has him back safe and sound.'

28 "The older brother became angry and refused to go in. So his father went out and pleaded with him. 29 But he answered his father, 'Look! All these years I've been slaving for you and never disobeyed your orders. Yet you never gave me even a young goat so I could celebrate with my friends. 30 But when this son of yours who has squandered your property with prostitutes comes home, you kill the fattened calf for him!'

31 "'My son,' the father said, 'you are always with me, and everything I have is yours. 32 But we had to celebrate and be glad, because this brother of yours was dead and is alive again; he was lost and is found.'"

The Younger Son

RELEASE

READ OR LISTEN TO LUKE 15:11–32. Pay special attention to the part of the story that concerns the younger son. You can refer to page 18.

In the time of Jesus, the division of an inheritance would normally only take place after a death. So, when the younger son asks his father for his share of the inheritance, it can mean only one thing: he is impatient for his father's passing. While not against the Torah (cf. Deut. 21:17 which apportions one-third of an estate to the younger son), this still speaks of some sort of rebellion. The younger son is expressing his desire for his father to step aside so he can take his place.

Here we see the younger son's attitude, which is driven by self-centered pride: "give me my share of the estate" (v. 12). The younger son does not seem to care how this affects anyone else. He breaks, not the law, but a relationship. He breaks his father's heart.

The word used for inheritance is used 14 times in the New Testament, but surprisingly, it is not the word used in verse 12. The word here is *ousia,* which simply means property or wealth. This is important. In Jesus's time, what a son or male family member inherited after the passing of the head of the home was not just the wealth of the home, but the family's responsibilities that went along with it as well. However, *ousia* does not denote this additional aspect of responsibility. It only means wealth. It means that the younger son only asked for the resources of his family and did not want to assume any relational obligations. He then cuts himself off from his roots and strikes out on his own. He throws away everything that identifies him in order to begin a new life in a far country (v. 13).

There "he squandered his wealth in wild living" (v. 13). We usually understand this to mean the younger son was behaving in acts of loose or immoral ways. And this is what the elder son believes when he later says that his brother spent his money on prostitutes (v. 30). However, an alternative understanding may be more in line with the customs of Jesus's day.

The word *squander* simply means "to scatter" (as in scattering an enemy in battle). We do not know how the younger son scattered his money. The elder son assumed it was with prostitutes, but he did not really know, and the parable is silent on the subject except to say it was on wild living. All we know was that the money was wasted.

> *what am I trying to do my own way?*

The adverb *wild* used by Jesus in verse 13 is only found here in the NT. The Arabic translations of this verse translate the word as *extravagant* living. This translation fits better for a traditional Middle East villager. In traditional village society, a person often spent their inheritance to establish a reputation and debt obligations. This was done by acts of generosity and hospitality. For example, by holding large banquets and giving expensive gifts, you established prestige and status, bought friendship, and accrued obligations from others. You became an important person in your community. In this sense, the younger son was trying to become his father but in his own way. (There are echoes here of Genesis 3 where humankind sought to be like God but in their own way.)

However, "after he had spent everything, there was a severe famine" (a great horror in the ancient world) and the son "began to be in need" (v. 14). He was alone, destitute, and starving, desperately needing help. Kenneth Baily proposed the situation like this. If the son had anyone owing him favors, he might have tried to call them in. In an honor and shame culture, which was the culture of Jesus's day, the prodigal son would have gone to those who owed him and asked for help. One could not refuse to help since they owed an obligation. However, if one did not or could not help, what would you do? You would offer something that you knew the person you owed a debt to would refuse to accept—thereby addressing an obligation at no cost to yourself without losing face.[7]

In this case, what would a good Jewish boy be almost certain of not agreeing to do? Why, tending pigs. According to the Torah, pigs were unclean animals. But surprisingly, the son is so desperate, he accepts the job. In fact, Jesus says he was in such a bad condition that he "longed" (v. 16) for the pig pods. The word for *longing* here is an intense word of deep emotion. Jesus also used it in the Last Supper when he said he greatly desired to eat the Passover meal with his disciples (Luke 22:15).

The prodigal longed to be a pig so he could eat the pods the pigs were eating.

Then, coming to his senses (v. 17) he decides to return home to throw himself on the mercy of his father. But, since the relationship had been broken, he knows he cannot go home as a son only as a servant (v. 19). What a role reversal. At the beginning of the parable, the prodigal wanted to be like his father, but at this point he can only aspire to eat pig's food and be a slave.

> *Let's pause at this point to consider our own journey in life.*
>
> *Where do we find ourselves like the younger son?*
>
> *Where do we need to come to our senses?*

The answer to our own self-pride and desire to live on our own is also to repent and turn back. We need to learn to *release* and let go of the false self and all our strivings. Before we can receive from the Father, we too need to surrender our pride, ambitions, desires, and strivings. Before God can fill us, we need to empty ourselves. Where do you need to let go and release yourself to the Father?

The Open/Closed Fist Exercise

To help illustrate our struggles when we hold too tightly to things or people instead of releasing them to God, we invite you to hold out your hand.

> *Close your fist tightly and feel what it is like as you continue to hold the tension.*

What does it feel like? (pause)

> » *You might be aware of tightness and the draining of physical strength, or even emotional strength.*

How conscious are you of other parts of your body? (pause)

Can you concentrate on other things and still tightly clench your fist? (pause)

> » *You might be aware that holding your fist tightly closed would affect your ability to respond to other gestures or movement toward you.*

If someone were to come to you and wanted something, would you be able to give it to them? (pause)

What if someone came to shake your hand? Would you be able to take it?

Now, slowly let your fist become relaxed and open your fist. Notice the difference between the two states: closed and open.

What are you feeling now?

Are you now able to pay attention to something else?

When we are unable to let go, we cannot receive anything else. We often hold on tightly because we are afraid or are angry. We fear losing something we do not want to lose. Or maybe we are angry and clench our fists to fight back. But God does not want us to be fearful or angry people. He wants us to relinquish control of our lives to Him. He wants to us to be free people, to be more like Jesus.

The next section contains a series of questions for you to reflect on concerning release. Please do not feel you need to hurry through or to answer all the questions. Only use them as a guide to help you converse with God about any areas that He might be asking you to let go of. At the end of the section is another exercise which you may want to do. Please plan for at least ten minutes for this last exercise (use a name tag included in your material or on the last page of the questions).

Pull away now and separate from others in silence and solitude. Take the next hour to reflect on the younger son and what he had to let go of in order to return to the father. Ask God to help you release and surrender whatever is holding you back from opening your heart wide to the Lord who loves you and calls you back to His loving embrace.

Release

RELEASE | *"to free from anything that restrains; to free from confinement, bondage, pain; to let go; to give up; relinquish, or surrender (a right, claim, etc.)."* [8]

REFLECT & PONDER

This section contains a series of questions for you to individually reflect on around release. Please do not feel you need to hurry through or to answer all the questions. Use them as a guide to help you converse with God about any areas that He might be asking you to let go of.

At the end of this section is another exercise.
Please plan for at least ten minutes for this last exercise.

Pull away now and separate from others in silence and solitude. Take the next hour to reflect on the younger son and what he had to let go of in order to return to the Father. Ask God to help you release and surrender whatever is holding you back from opening your heart wide to the Lord who loves you and calls you back to His loving embrace.

Let us throw off everything that hinders and the sin that so easily entangles.

Herbrews 12:1

Have this attitude in yourselves, which was also in Christ Jesus, who, as He already existed in the form of God, did not consider equality with God a thing to be grasped, but emptied Himself.

Philippians 2:5–7, NASB

Reflection

Before God can do His work within us, what kinds of things might you need to release so that God can give you more of Himself? For example:

> *Regret, shame, guilt*

> *Worry, anxiety, fear*

> *Insecurity, inadequacy, need*

> *Your own attitudes*

> *Your own plans or agenda*

> *Addictive behaviors that comfort or distract*

> *Searching for love in the wrong places*

> *Your outward or inward sins*

PONDER

Where are you living with clenched fists? What would it look like to open your hands?

Where does *release* seem most relevant right now?

What do you need to release to God? (relationships, performance, future direction, hopes, health, finances)

What sin areas might you need to confess and ask forgiveness for? What addictions to this world do you need to recognize and release?

In ***The Return of the Prodigal Son,*** Henri Nouwen says that receiving forgiveness requires a total willingness "to let God be God and do all the healing, restoring, and renewing."[9] How might you be trying to heal yourself without asking God's help?

Nouwen also says we are like the younger son every time we search for unconditional love where it cannot be found.[10] Where are you searching for unconditional love outside the Father's heart?

Where do you find your identity? Take some time to be open and honest with yourself.

Nouwen also says that Jesus became the true prodigal son for our sake. "He left the house of His Heavenly Father, came to a foreign country, gave away all that he had, and returned through the cross to His Father's home."[11] All of this He did not do as a rebellious son, but as an obedient one. In Rembrandt's picture, imagine the younger son representing all of humanity's return to the Father through the cross of Christ. Ponder this image. Record your thoughts.

Exercise

Save at least ten minutes for this last exercise.
Take one of the name tages provided (or use the box below).

> *Sit in silence before the Lord.*
> *Try to simply be present with Him and allow Him to be present with you.*

When you come to a sense of stillness, look at the name tag and ask God to reveal to you the false names you have lived with to this point in your life.

> » *If it helps, write them down on a separate piece of paper. When you are done, look or think over your list. Is there one that stands out?*

Write this down on your name tag.

Ask God to reveal to you how living out that name has affected your life and how that name still affects you today.

> » *Now take that name tag and tear it to pieces or cross out the name symbolizing your release from that false identity.*

Listen deeply as God tells you: *This is not your name.*

Name Tag

Debrief

GROUP | Come back together after your time of solitude. Divide into small groups of three or four, preferably gender specific. Take 30 minutes to share what the Lord has been revealing to you on your younger son side or what you need to release. Pray for one another during this time.

INDIVIDUAL | Spend this time recording your thoughts in your journal or on this page. Talk to the Lord about what He has been revealing to you about what you need to release to Him.

The Elder Son

RECEIVE

READ OR LISTEN to the parable in Luke 15:11–32 again, but this time focus on the elder son's part of the story. You can refer to page 18.

It is good to remind ourselves of the audience to whom Jesus is telling this parable. In Luke 15:1–2, Luke records the context of the stories he shares in the chapter: "Now the tax collectors and sinners were all gathering around to hear Jesus. But the Pharisees and the teachers of the law muttered, 'This man welcomes sinners and eats with them.'"

The Pharisees and the elders were the focus audience for the prodigal parable. Like the elder son, they too needed to learn of the Father's unconditional love for sinners. Two points should be noted.

First, Luke wanted to make sure we understand who is being illustrated by the elder son. The word for the elder son in verse 25 is *presbyteros,* which is used as the title for the elders of the people. In the Gospels this occurs most frequently in conjunction with the scribes or teachers of the law as is in verse 2 (cf. Matt. 27:41; Mark 11:22, 14:43,53; Luke 20:1). There is no mistaking who the elder son represents.

Second, the Pharisees and scribes *muttered* about Jesus eating with sinners. This is the same word used in the Septuagint (the Greek Old Testament) to describe the complaints of Israel in the wilderness (cf. Exodus 15:24, 16:2,7–8, 17:3; Numbers 14:2, 16:11). The Israelites muttered against God then, and the Pharisees muttered against Jesus now. The connection is complete.

As to the parable itself, we see in verse 25, that the elder son returned from the fields and heard commotion happening at home. It is very possible, according to Bailey, that the elder son knew exactly what was going on for there were usually no secrets in village life.¹² But whether or not he knew his brother had come home, he called over a nearby servant (though the word used here simply means a youth) and asked him what was happening. The boy was probably one of people singing and dancing outside the home. "'Your brother has come,' he replied, 'and your father has killed the fattened calf because he has him back safe and sound'" (v. 27).

The words *safe* and *sound* are translated from the word *hygiano* (we get hygiene from it) which is often translated from Hebrew as *Shalom,* meaning wholeness and peace. The younger son has returned and is now at peace, reconciled with the Father—whole again. This causes the elder son to explode in anger (v. 28) and he refuses to go into the home and to accept his brother's return. He accuses his father of feasting with his brother, a sinner (vv. 29–30). This is the very thing that the Pharisees accuse Jesus of, eating with sinners, at the beginning of the chapter in verse 2.

And now we have the most tender aspect of the parable and something we often do not notice in the story. Verse 28 tells us that the "father went out and pleaded with him." In an honor and shame culture, a son would not ask his father to approach him. If he had a problem, it would be his responsibility and requirement to approach his father. But here the father is willing to be shamed in order to seek reconciliation with his elder son. The father gives costly and self-emptying love to be with his son.

you only need to receive

The word Luke used for *plead* is a combination of the verb *kleto,* meaning "to call" and the prefix *para* meaning "with" or "alongside." *Kleto* can have other prefixes, like *en* "against," or *pro,* meaning "attack" which would indicate a more hostile attitude. But here *parakleto* denotes a desire to call to reconcile. This is supported by the word the father calls his son, *teknon* (the common word for son is *huios*). *Teknon* has a deeply affectionate meaning, like, "my dearest son." These things communicate the father comes only in love to his eldest son, seeking to reconcile.

And what does the father say to defuse his son's anger, resentfulness, bitterness, jealousy, and self-pity? He says, "My son ... you are always with me, and everything I have is yours" (v. 31). Or, in other words, "I am not holding anything back from you—you only need to ***receive.***" The problem the elder son had was not that he was neglected or passed over, but that he had forgotten to receive from his father. Everything was his, he just had to ask and receive what the father was so willing to give.

It is interesting that the parable is left unfinished. Jesus leaves the account in midair. We never know if the elder son repents of his anger and returns home like his brother. We never know if he opens his hands to receive what the father says has always been his. This was probably intentional, demanding we consider our own willingness to receive.

By identifying the elder son with the Pharisees and Scribes that surrounded him, Jesus was pleading with them in gentle terms to also return to the Father and be welcomed home in His love. It is doubtful that many in the crowd changed their hearts and embraced both Jesus and the sinners that he ate with.

But what about us? Let us consider how this parable might reflect our own elder brother attitudes. One way to quiet and open our hearts to receive the good gifts the Lord has in store for us is to allow our own body rhythms to match our heart desires. To do this, we want to introduce a prayer traditionally called Breath Prayer. You pray short prayers in alignment with your breathing. The breath prayer has its roots in the Psalms (cf. Psalm 139:1). The church father, Gregory of Sinai, says, "One's love of God should run before breathing."[13]

Breath Prayer Exercise

Breath prayer is discerned more than created. When we pray a breath prayer, we are asking God to show us our posture before Him. To do this, we need to quiet ourselves before the Lord.

Take a few minutes to sit in silence, slowing our breathing and, if possible, our heart rate.

» *Picture yourself being held in God's loving presence.*

After a few moments allow yourself to hear God call you by name.

» *Next, let this question surface:*

"What do I want to receive?"

» *Answer the question simply and directly.*

Maybe a single word comes to mind, like faith, joy, love, etc., or a phrase, like, "to understand your will," "to feel your love," etc.

Next, connect this word or phrase with the most comfortable way you have of addressing God, such as, "Blessed Savior," "Father God," "Abba," etc.

» *Finally, you may want to write your breath prayer, staying within what is comfortable to say in one breath. Here are some examples:*

> *Father (inhale); Thank You (exhale).*
>
> *I cannot earn it (inhale); I can only receive it (exhale).*
>
> *My heart is troubled (inhale); I receive your Peace (exhale).*
>
> *I cast my cares (inhale); Upon you, O Lord (exhale).*
>
> *You are enough (inhale); so, I am enough (exhale).*

» *Opening your hands, as if receiving, while you close your eyes may be helpful as you pray.*

Receive

RECEIVE | *"to take into one's possession; to have (something) bestowed, conferred, etc.; to have delivered (something) or brought to one."*[14]

REFLECT & PONDER

Take the next hour with the Lord and away from others. Ask yourself how you are like the elder son and reflect on the questions that follow, again only using them as a guide to your conversation with the Lord. Notice that God graciously allowed us to catch a glimpse into his heart as he pleads with his eldest son to come home. God desires to reconcile with those places in us that are distant or preoccupied. He mourns when we do not draw near to him and receive all that he wants to give us. He grieves when we forget him in the muchness and manyness of our lives. He longs for our presence.

> ***What does the Father want to give you today?***

He came to that which was his own, but his own did not receive him. Yet to all who did receive him, to those who believed in his name, he gave the right to become the children of God—children born not of natural descent, nor of human decision or a husband's will, but born of God.

John 1:11–13

Reflection

> *Receiving requires a certain posture of open hands. It is a posture of expectancy and requires us to believe in something. To believe that God is always working.*

> *We also need a posture of attentiveness. God often comes in ways and forms that we do not expect or are not looking for, and, so, we must be attentive to the ways of the Word and Spirit.*

> *In fact, we cannot control how or where or when the Spirit will come (John 3:8); that is where the waiting comes in. Waiting is an essential part of the receiving.*

> *Receiving is not something that can be achieved or accomplished, or even earned; by its very nature it is something that can only be given or conferred. It is a gift. All attention is on the one giving the gift because it focuses on the heart of the giver.*

> *However, the most important part of the receiving is to take hold of whatever we have received and make it our own. We must get our hands on it, take hold of it, and make it our own.*

> *One gift given/gifted upon us is a new name (Isaiah 62:2; Revelation 3:12). We wait in eager anticipation to receive God's new name for us.*

PONDER

How might you be trying to live the life of the elder son by trying to meet expectations and to be seen as obedient and dutiful? Where has service become a burden to you? What might that mean?

Like the elder son, where in your life might you be holding onto jealousy, bitterness, resentfulness, judgment, condemnation, pride, or anger?

In ***The Return of the Prodigal Son,*** Henri Nouwen says that complaining is "self-perpetuating and counterproductive" and that the experience of the resentful heart is the experience of not being able to enter fully into the Father's joy.[15] Where has complaining robbed you of the joy of the Father?

The Father wants not only his younger son but his elder son back too. Where is the Father running out to meet your elder son spirit? Where does He invite you to go back inside your home?

What are you most deeply longing to receive from God?

What helps you be more receptive to Him? What is your biggest obstacle to receiving from Him?

How is the word *receive* most relevant to you right now?

What do you need to believe in order to receive from the Father?

Where might God already be working in your life, wanting to give you something you may have not even recognized?

Are there any areas where might you be trying to take matters into your own hands and trying to make something happen rather than waiting for the Father's answers?

Exercise

Save at least ten minutes for this last exercise.
Take one of the name tages provided (or use the box below).

> **Pause and find quiet before the Lord.**

» *Turn to Isaiah 62 and read teh passage. Read it slowly with listening ears.*

Pay careful attention to anything that resonates within you. When something strikes a chord within you, stop, and pay attention to what God is saying.

Notice the names in the passage. Which ones connect with your heart?

Ask God to reveal a name to you for your life situation right now.

» *Write that name on the name tag and put it on your chest (or save it on the paper below). Listen to Him speak that name to you over and over.*

Name Tag

Debrief

GROUP | Come back together after your time of solitude. Divide up into small groups of three or four, preferably gender specific. Take 30 minutes to share what the Lord has been revealing to you on your younger son side or your need to release. Pray for one another during this time.

INDIVIDUAL | Spend this time recording your thoughts in your journal or on this page. Talk to the Lord about what He has been revealing to you about what you need to release to Him.

Meal Break

After group sharing around the elder son is complete, it's time to pause for a meal break. We encourage groups to eat in a silent and reflective mood to not break the atmosphere of quiet we have been experiencing. However, we can be joyful in contemplative fellowship.

Depending on the size of the group, the mealtime can take anywhere from half an hour to one hour. If possible, it would be good to have a simple already-prepared meal laid out for people to help themselves to. Some groups ask outside help to serve them by preparing and serving the meal.

The Father

REST

LISTEN OR READ Luke 15:11–32 one more time. This time focus and listen to the father's part of the story. You can refer to page 18.

While this parable is known as the parable of the prodigal son, the father—the God figure in the story—is the main character in the story. In this way we could call this parable the parable of the compassionate father and the two lost sons.

In the beginning of the parable, when the younger son requested his inheritance, it showed his desire for his father not to be around anymore. Then he used his inheritance unwisely and was left with nothing but the thought of returning home to serve as a household slave. The younger son is lost.

A Middle East scholar, Kenneth Bailey explained a well-known ceremony called a ***kezazah*** (literally "the cutting off" in Arabic) to help us understand what might have been happening here.

In Jesus's time, custom dictated that if a Jewish boy lost the family inheritance among the Gentiles and dared to return home, the community would break a large pot in front of him and cry out the person's name saying, "So and so is cut off from his people."[16]

After they performed this ceremony, the community or village would have nothing to do with him until restitution of the inheritance was made.

And the only way restitution could be made in this honor and shame culture was if, just as with this parable, the younger son was to pay back his debt to his father in full. This had to be accomplished through a mediator, because the father would never shame himself to meet his son until restitution was made.[17]

So, who was the mediator? It was not the village elder or even someone who might possess necessary negotiating skills. In the middle east, relationship was paramount, so the mediator was always the closest relative. In the parable, this would have been the elder son. However, as we have seen, the elder son refused to even entertain the idea of welcoming his younger brother home, let alone to serve as a helper in restoring his relationship with their father. And so, in this sense, the elder son was also lost in his own resentfulness.

Since the usual course would be for the son to approach the father through a mediator to seek payment of his debt obligation and the younger son knew this was something he could never do, this explains the younger son's statement as he realizes his situation, "I am no longer worthy to be called your son; make me like one of your hired servants (v. 19).

And then something amazing happens. While the son is still a long way off, the father sees him and, rather than wait for mediation that is expected and the father is entitled to, he "was filled with compassion for him; he ran to his son, threw his arms around him and kissed him (v. 20). The word *kiss (katephilesen)* means either "kissed again and again" or "to kiss tenderly." By showing such affection the father is taking the initiative in expressing his deep love for the son.

> *for the father to do this first was countercultural*

There is also a significant point that Luke is making when he says the father runs (the word used means "sprint") to his son. As we have pointed out, in that culture it was up to the son to approach his father to beg for reconciliation. For the father to do this first without waiting for his son's apology was countercultural. Also, running in a long robe could only be accomplished by lifting the garment up over the knees. To expose one's naked legs, man or woman, was a shameful act in that culture. The father took shame upon himself by running to his son. This was not how you should act in such a society (and remember, this was all done publicly). By doing so he showed his compassion and deep love through this costly self-giving.

At the conclusion of the parable, the prodigal is enjoying table fellowship with the father in a celebratory feast (v. 27). He is home. He is found (v. 32). He is at rest.

We can gladly see the comparison between the father's costly love for his son in the parable and Jesus's own costly self-giving on the cross for us. At the Last Supper, Phillip asks Jesus to show them the Father (John 14:8). And Jesus responds: "Anyone who has seen me has seen the Father" (v. 9). Jesus is telling us He loves like the Father. His love brought him to earth and brought him to the cross. Like the father in the parable, Jesus comes running to us and says: "Come to me, all who are weary and burdened, and I will give you rest" (Matt. 11:28).

he is home.
he is found.
he is at rest.

The Father wants to give us rest through our faith in Jesus Christ and what Jesus did for us on the cross. We find rest when we let go and return (younger son) to the Father and then receive all that he has for us (elder son).

Resting in the Love of the Father Exercise

Take a piece of paper or the following page and the colored pencils that are provided.

> *Close your eyes, quiet your thoughts, and open your heart and mind to God. Imagine what it would be like to rest in his unconditional love.*

PLAY THE SONG | "Oh, the Deep, Deep Love of Jesus" and allow time to ponder Jesus's love for you. We recommend Audrey Assad's version of *Oh, the Deep, Deep Love of Jesus*.

> » *As you listen to the song, when you are ready, start by writing "Resting in the Father's Love" across the top of the page, then draw how you might imagine resting in the Father's arms.*

How does it feel?

What might it look like for you?

What thoughts come to mind?

> » *Do not worry about whether or not you are skilled in drawing. You might want your picture only to be symbolic or made only of colors. Take your time. It's okay if you don't finish the picture during the song.*

After listening to the song and drawing your picture, as we have done in the previous sections, you can continue in quiet reflective work for the next hour using the next Reflect & Ponder section on **rest**.

Rest

REST | *"to be at ease, have tranquility or peace; to be quiet or still; refreshing ease, relief, or freedom, especially from anything that wearies, troubles, or disturbs; a period of interval of inactivity, response, solitude, or tranquility; mental or spiritual calm."* [18]

REFLECT & PONDER

This section contains a series of questions for you to reflect on around rest. Please do not feel you need to hurry through or to answer all the questions. Use them as a guide to help you converse with God about any areas that He might be asking you to enter into His rest.

Let the beloved of the Lord rest secure in him, for he shields him all day long, and the one the Lord loves rests between his shoulders.

Deuteronomy 33:12

In repentance and rest is your salvation, in quietness and trust is your strength.

Isaiah 30:15

Reflection

> The last stage of the spiritual journey is sometimes called coming to rest or union with Christ.

> This is the place we most deeply long for, the silent embrace of two lovers.

> This embrace fully convinces us that our worth and value lies in the love-filled heart of our Savior.

> Once we are at rest in Him, the wholeness, the fullness, and the life that we were created for can be fully experienced.

> Our rest, therefore, does not come from completing activities but upon the knowledge of being fully known and loved by our Father.

> True rest depends upon trust in God alone—not through our efforts.

> True rest depends on this trust and then belief—belief that God is both strong and powerful enough to protect us and everything that concerns us as we rest in Him.

> Rest results when we focus on what is profoundly important, not what is momentarily urgent.

PONDER

What is your first reaction to the word *rest?*

When in your life have you experienced genuine rest—physical, emotional, or spiritual?

What is the biggest obstacle in your life to rest? What keeps you from resting in His loving embrace?

What does the above answer reveal to you about your belief and value systems?

The true center of Rembrandt's painting is the hands of the father—mercy becoming flesh. We have the image of a very old man, crying tenderly, blessing his deeply wounded son. What does this image show about God's love for you?

How does comparing yourself to others distract from the love that God wants you to receive from Him and rest in?

In ***The Return of the Prodigal Son,*** Henri Nouwen discussed the Father's love by saying that the question is not, How do I find, know, and love God? but How does God find, know, and love me?[19] Meditate on that statement. What does it say to you about your need to rest in the Father's love and your present relationship with Jesus?

At the close of the parable of the prodigal, there is a celebration. God delighting over His returned child. This is an invitation to joy between you and the Father. How might God be inviting you into joy with Him?

Exercise

Stay in your quiet place for a few minutes longer and settle into silence as you sit before the Lord of the universe.

Resist any words that might come to your mind and simply relax into the Father's arms.

» *Do this for ten minutes and then record your thoughts below or in your journal.*

Listen to His heartbeat.

Look into His eyes.

Listen for His voice.

Feel His deep love.

Closing

REFLECT & SHARE

GROUPS | Rather than dividing up in small groups for this last section, we encourage you to come together as a large group and share with one another what the Lord has been revealing to you specifically during your time with Him.

DISCUSSION OPTIONS

- Share your picture of what it means to be resting in the Father's Love.
- Further discuss Rembrandt's painting.
- Share a specific answer to a question in any of the three sections on **release**, **receive**, or **rest**. Share something that you sense God is inviting you into or share a prayer request.

Make sure the print of the painting is still displayed for group

If you are the leader of the retreat, as participants share, have them come to the table that has been prepared in front. On the table is a dish with hearts. After sharing, have each participant pick up a heart from the dish to symbolize what the Lord has spoken to them about the Father's heart during this retreat. As people return home, mention that they can put this heart in a place where they can see it to be a reminder of how much God loves them.

PLAY THE SONG

After everyone who wants to share has finished and after everyone has collected their hearts (whether they share publicly or not), we will close the retreat by listening to the song "When God Ran," by Phillips, Craig and Dean. Or a second option would be to play the music video. [20]

When the song ends, we will pray the Litergy of Leave Taking and depart in fellowship and joy.

The Liturgy of Leave Taking

Leader: Here at day's end, we seek you, O King of Earth and Heaven.

All: *You have been our sustenance across the day's hours.*

Leader: Be now our counselor, comforter, and protector as we depart from this blessed time with one another this day.

All: *Amen.*

Leader: We now give thanks for the blessings of the day that has passed.

All: *[Individually as lead, offer up short thanksgivings to where and how God has met you on this day. Praise Him in thanksgiving.]*

Leader: To gather joyfully is indeed a serious affair. So, as we depart let it be to us also a delight and a glad foretaste of His eternal kingdom.

All: *Bless us, O Lord, as we linger together and into this evening as we relish what you have given to us today. May this day fall like a great hammer blow against the brittle night to come, shattering the gloom, reawakening our hearts, stirring imaginations, focusing our vision on the kingdom of heaven that is to come, on the kingdom that is promised, on the kingdom that is already, indeed, among us.*

Leader: Take joy, O King!

All: *Take joy!*

Leader: All will be well!

All: *All will be well! Nothing good and right and true will be lost forever. All good things will be restored. Take joy, my friends, take joy!*

Leader: Now, you who are loved by the Father, prepare your hearts, and give yourselves wholly with open hands to the rest and gifts you are to receive, to the glad company of the saints, to the comforting fellowship of the Spirit, and to the abiding presence of Christ, who is seated both among us and with His Father in heaven.

All: *Amen.*

Leader: In the name of the Father, the Son, and the Holy Spirit, go in peace.21

NOTES

1. Barton, *Invitation to Retreat*, 11.

2. Barton, *Invitation to Retreat*, 126.

3. Adapted from Pickering, *Creative Ideas for Quiet Days*, 77.

4. R. C. Trench, *Notes on the Parables of our Lord*, 387.

5. Bailey, *The Cross & the Prodigal*, 87–88.

6. Bailey, *The Cross & the Prodigal*, 87–88.

7. Bailey, *The Cross & the Prodigal*, 55–57.

8. Branch, *Becoming*, 31. Some of the questions for reflection in all three sections are also adapted from Branch's book.

9. Nouwen, *The Return of the Prodigal Son*, 53.

10. Nouwen, *The Return of the Prodigal Son*, 43.

11. Nouwen, *The Return of the Prodigal Son*, 55.

12. Bailey, *The Cross & the Prodigal*, 79.

13. St. Gregory of Sinai, *The Philokalia*, 285.

14. Branch, *Becoming*, 50.

15. Nouwen, *The Return of the Prodigal Son*, 72.

16. Bailey, *The Cross & the Prodigal* 52–53

17. See Bailey, *The Cross & the Prodigal*, 52–53. We are indebted to Bailey's commentary for the middle eastern cultural understanding of the parable.

18. Branch, *Becoming*, 79.

19. Nouwen, *The Return of the Prodigal Son*, 106.

20. YouTube Music Video: https://www.youtube.com/watch?v=1Akv2V5fNdk

21. Adapted from Douglas Kaine McKelvey, *Every Moment Holy*, 8 & 112–116. Used by permission.

BIBLIOGRAPHY

Bailey, Kenneth E. *The Cross & the Prodigal: Luke 15 Through the Eyes of Middle Eastern Peasants.* Downers Grove: IVP, 2005.

Barton, Ruth Haley. *Invitation to Retreat: The Gift and Necessity of Time Away with God.* Downers Grove: IVP Books, 2018.

Branch, Jim. *Becoming.* Createspace Independent Publishing Platform, 2013.

Durham, John I. *The Biblical Rembrandt: Human Painter in a Landscape of Faith.* Macon: Mercer university Press, 2004.

St Nikodimos of the Holy Mountain and St Makarios of Corinth. *The Philokalia: The Complete Text,* vol. 4. Edited and translated by G. E. H. Palmer, Philip Sherrard. , and Kallistos Ware, *complied by* London: Faber & Faber, 1998, 207–287.

McKelvey, Douglas Kaine, and Ned Bustard. *Every Moment Holy,* vol. 1. Nashville: Rabbit Room Press, 2017.

Nouwen, Henri J. M. *The Return of the Prodigal Son.* New York: Doubleday & Co., Inc, 1992.

Pickering, Sue. *Creative Ideas for Quiet Days: Resources and Liturgies for Retreats and Days of Reflection.* Norwich: Canterbury Press, 2006.

Trench, R. C. *Notes on the Parables of our Lord.* London: John W. Parker, 1857.

Discography

Assad, Audrey, feat. Fernando Ortega. 2016. "Oh, the Deep, Deep Love of Jesus." Track 6 on *Inheritance,* Fortunate Fall Records.

Chapman, Steven Curtis. 1999. "Be Still and Know." Track 13 on *Speechless,* Sparrow Records.

Phillips, Craig and Dean. 1992. "When God Ran." Track 4 on *Restoration.* Sparrow Records.

Available Online

For use on iPad or Kindle

amazonkindle